CRIME SOLVERS

FINGERPRINT EVIDENCE

by Amy Kortuem

CAPSTONE PRESS
a capstone imprint

Blazers Books are published by Capstone Press,
1710 Roe Crest Drive, North Mankato, Minnesota 56003
www.mycapstone.com

Library of Congress Cataloging-in-Publication Data
Names: Kortuem, Amy, author.
Title: Fingerprint evidence / by Amy Kortuem.
Description: North Mankato, Minnesota : Capstone Press, [2019] | Series:
    Blazers. Crime solvers. | Includes index.
Identifiers: LCCN 2018001964 (print) | LCCN 2018004525 (ebook) | ISBN
    9781543529968 (eBook PDF) | ISBN 9781543529883 (hardcover) | ISBN
    9781543529920 (pbk.)
Subjects: LCSH: Fingerprints—Juvenile literature. | Criminal
    investigation—Juvenile literature.
Classification: LCC HV6074 (ebook) | LCC HV6074 .K676 2019 (print) | DDC
    363.25/8—dc23
LC record available at https://lccn.loc.gov/2018001964

Editorial Credits
Carrie Braulick Sheely, editor; Kayla Rossow, designer; Svetlana Zhurkin,
media researcher; Kris Wilfahrt, production specialist

Photo Credits
Alamy: Jochen Tack, 19, Mikael Karlsson, 17, PA Images, 5; AP Photo:
Charlie Neibergall, 23; Courtesy of the Federal Bureau of Investigations, 21;
Dreamstime: Jcuneok, 9; Getty Images: Hero Images, 28–29; iStockphoto:
D-Keine, 15; Newscom: imageBROKER/Jochen Tack, 7, Sipa Press/Valerie
Macon, 13, 22, Zuma Press/Douglas R. Clifford, 25, 26; Shutterstock: alexandre
zveiger, 12, Andrey Burmakin, 10 (top right), Corepics VOF, 18, Hans-Joachim
Roy, 10 (middle), JT Platt, 11, Presslab, 20, Torin55, 10 (top left), Zoka74, cover,
16; Svetlana Zhurkin, 14

Design Elements by Shutterstock

Printed in the United States.
PA017

TABLE OF CONTENTS

Chapter 1

At the Crime Scene. 4

Chapter 2

Fingerprint Features 8

Chapter 3

Gathering Fingerprint Evidence 14

Chapter 4

Finding Matches. 20

Glossary 30

Read More 31

Internet Sites 31

Critical Thinking Questions 32

Index 32

At the Crime Scene

A store owner reports a robbery. Crime **scene** investigators (CSIs) rush to the store. They look for clues the robbers left behind.

scene—the place of an event or action

^ CSIs are some of the first investigators
to arrive at crime scenes.

A CSI brushes dark powder on a door handle. The powder makes fingerprints appear. Workers later find the prints match those of a **criminal**. Fingerprint **evidence** helps solve another crime.

criminal—someone who commits a crime

evidence—information, items, and facts that help prove something is true or false; criminal evidence can be used in court cases

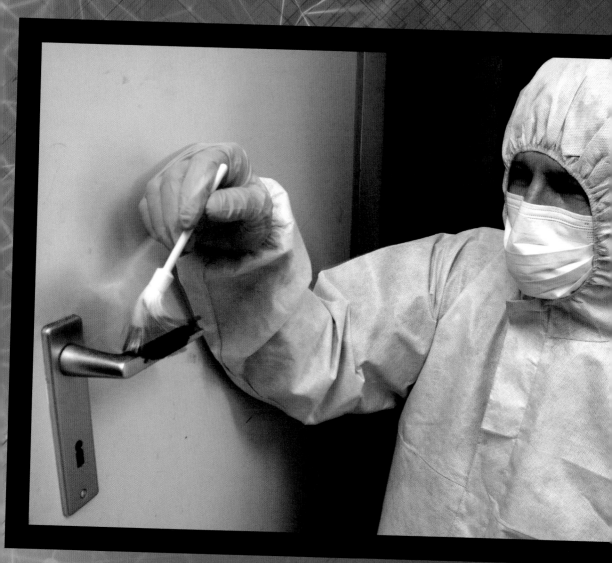

CSIs often dust powder on surfaces that are most likely to have fingerprints, such as door handles.

CHAPTER 2

Fingerprint Features

The skin inside our hands is covered with ridges. Everyone's fingers have different ridge patterns. Sweat and oil stick to the ridges. When we touch objects, the sweat and oil is left behind as fingerprints.

finger ridges

FACT

Not even identical twins have the same
ridge patterns on their fingers.

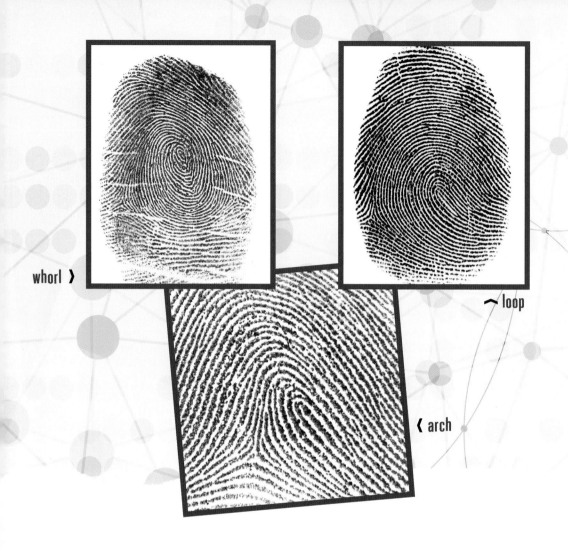

whorl >

~ loop

< arch

People have three main types of
fingerprint patterns. They are arches,
whorls, and loops. An arch looks like an
upside-down U or V. A whorl is a spiral.
In a loop, ridges enter on one side. They
then curve and go back to the same side.

gorilla hand

FACT

Gorillas, chimpanzees, and koalas have fingerprints.
Koala fingerprints are very similar to human prints.

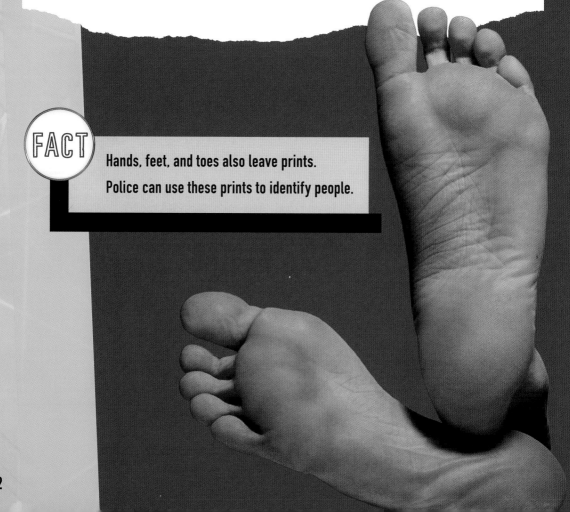

Tiny details make fingerprints different from one another. Ridges start or stop at ends. Ridges that split and come back together are called enclosures.

FACT

Hands, feet, and toes also leave prints. Police can use these prints to identify people.

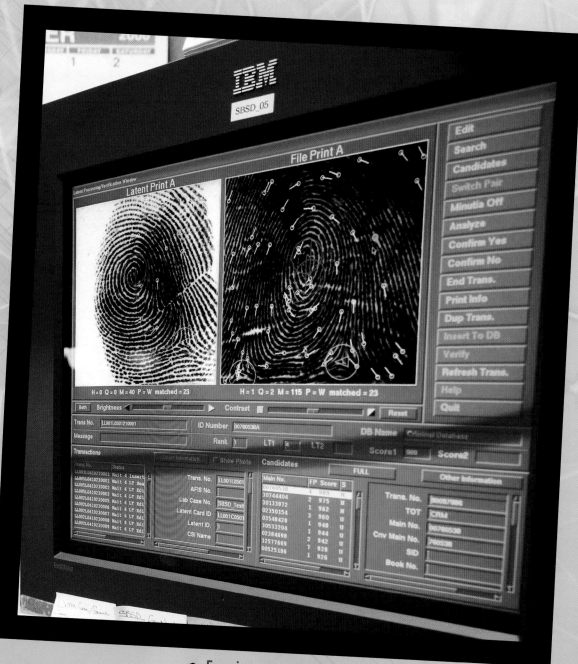

^ Examiners use fingerprint details to compare prints. The red circles mark details of each print.

CHAPTER 3

Gathering Fingerprint Evidence

⌃ plastic fingerprints in wax

CSIs look for different types of fingerprints at crime scenes. Bloody or dirty fingers leave **patent** prints they can see easily. CSIs can also see **plastic** prints. These prints include those left in wet cement or wax.

FACT Fingerprints can last on surfaces for thousands of years. Scientists found fingerprints in the tomb of an Egyptian king named King Tut. King Tut's tomb is more than 3,000 years old.

➤ Bloody patent prints are left behind on a door frame.

patent—able to be seen easily

plastic—describes a fingerprint that is pressed into a soft or wet object; people can see plastic fingerprints with the naked eye

CSIs must develop **latent** fingerprints. Special lights can show these prints. Heated superglue gives off **fumes** that show prints. CSIs also can brush metal powder over objects to show hidden prints.

❮ Metal powder makes latent prints appear.

latent—hidden from sight; latent fingerprints need to be developed to be seen

fume—gas, smoke, or vapor given off by something burning or by chemicals

Workers can use a chemical called ninhydrin to see fingerprints on paper and cardboard. It can show fingerprints that are more than 50 years old.

Heat from an iron can make fingerprints appear on paper that has been coated with ninhydrin.

CSIs **record** the fingerprints they
find. They often photograph prints.
CSIs press tape over powdered prints.
They lift the tape and stick it to a card.
The card then shows the prints.

record—to give evidence
of something

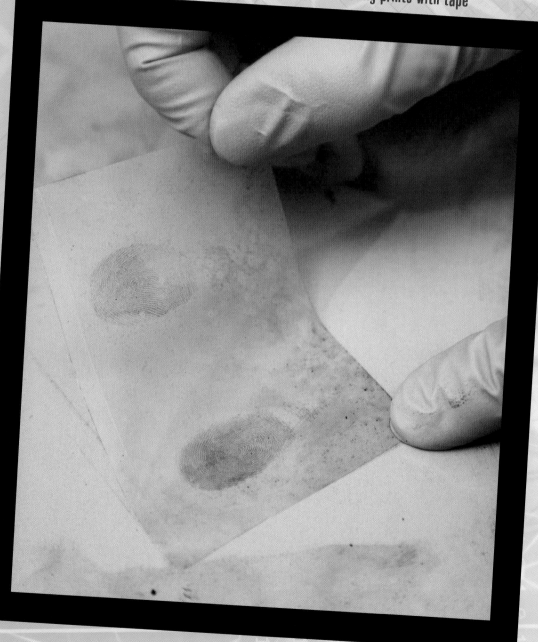

CHAPTER 4

Finding Matches

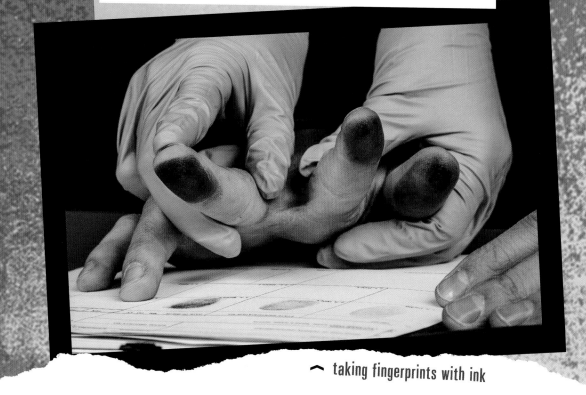

^ taking fingerprints with ink

Fingerprint examiners compare the saved fingerprints with others. Police may need to take people's fingerprints. This gives examiners prints to compare to the ones from the crime scene.

FACT

Fingerprint scanners can also help keep information on computers and other devices safe. The scanner can recognize your fingerprint. The device will stay locked unless your fingerprint is recognized.

^ A lab expert checks prints with an automated fingerprint identification system.

Examiners can enter fingerprint photos or **scans** from a crime scene into automated fingerprint identification systems. The U.S. national system is called the Next Generation Identification (NGI) system.

scan—a digital copy made for display or storage

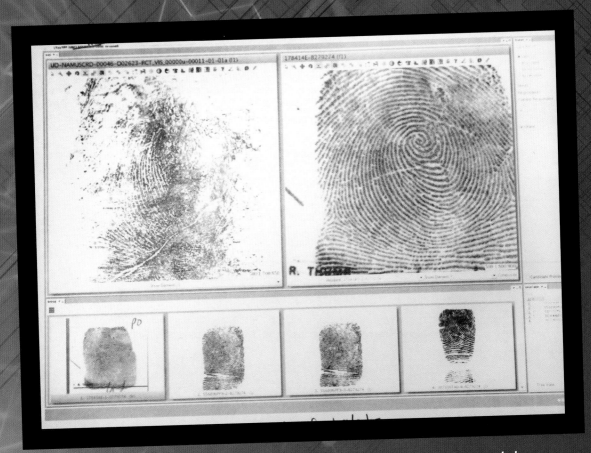

˄ A partial print from a dead body (left) matched the recorded fingerprint (right). Police were then able to identify the body.

The systems hold recorded prints of criminals and others. They look for fingerprints matching those from the crime scene. If there is a match, examiners study both sets of prints to check the match.

German company DERMALOG made the fastest automated fingerprint identification system in the world. It can process almost 1 billion prints per second.

An examiner studies prints at a fingerprint lab in Florida.

Automated fingerprint identification systems will continue to be a valuable tool for police.

Automated fingerprint identification systems continue to get faster and more accurate. The NGI system makes accurate matches more than 99 percent of the time.

FACT

Disney World scans the fingerprints of guests. The scans help make sure guests are using their own tickets.

People have used fingerprint evidence in American courts since 1911. Fingerprints are strong evidence in court cases. Many people have been found **guilty** of crimes based on them.

No crime-solving evidence is perfect. Some people have been freed from jail because of mistakes made while finding fingerprint matches.

guilty—found to be responsible for a crime

GLOSSARY

chemical (KE-muh-kuhl)—a substance used in or produced by chemistry; medicines, gunpowder, and food preservatives all are made from chemicals

criminal (KRI-muh-nuhl)—someone who commits a crime

evidence (EHV-uh-duhns)—information, items, and facts that help prove something is true or false; criminal evidence can be used in court cases

fume (FYOOM)—gas, smoke, or vapor given off by something burning or by chemicals

guilty (GIL-tee)—found to be responsible for a crime

latent (LAY-tuhnt)—hidden from sight; latent fingerprints need to be developed to be seen

patent (PAT-uhnt)—able to be seen with the naked eye; people can see patent fingerprints without developing them

plastic (PLASS-tik)—describes a fingerprint that is pressed into a soft or wet object

record (ree-KORD)—to give evidence of something

scan (SKAN)—a digital copy made for display or storage

scene (SEEN)—the place of an event or action

READ MORE

Carmichael, L. E. *Discover Forensic Science.* What's Cool About Science? Minneapolis: Lerner Publications, 2017.

Hanson, Anders. *Detective's Tools.* More Professional Tools. Minneapolis: ABDO, 2014.

Korté, Steve. *The Prints of Thieves: Batman & Robin Use Fingerprint Analysis to Crack the Case.* Batman & Robin Crime Scene Investigations. North Mankato, Minn.: Capstone, 2017.

INTERNET SITES

Use FactHound to find Internet sites related to this book.

Visit *www.facthound.com*

Just type in **9781543529883** and go.

Check out projects, games and lots more at
www.capstonekids.com

CRITICAL THINKING QUESTIONS

1. What skills do you think are important for CSIs to have? What could happen if CSIs didn't have these skills?

2. What is one main fingerprint type? How is this type different from the other two main types?

3. Why do you think fingerprints are one of the most trusted types of evidence?

INDEX

automated fingerprint identification systems, 22, 24, 27
    Next Generation Identification system, 22, 23, 27

courts, 28
criminals, 6, 24

enclosures, 12
ends, 12

fingerprint patterns, 10
    arches, 10
    loops, 10
    whorls, 10

latent fingerprints, 16

ninhydrin, 17

patent fingerprints, 14
plastic fingerprints, 14
powder, 6, 16, 18

ridge patterns, 8, 9, 10, 12

superglue, 16

taking fingerprints, 20